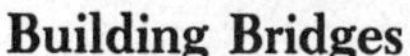

Building Bridges

BUILDING BRIDGES

Cos H. Davis, Jr.

BROADMAN PRESS
Nashville, Tennessee

Unless otherwise stated, all Scripture quotations are from the King James Version of the Bible. Scripture quotations marked NASB are from the *New American Standard Bible.* Copyright © The Lockman Foundation, 1960, 1962, 1963, 1968, 1971, 1972, 1973, 1975, 1977. Used by permission.

Library of Congress Cataloging in Publication Data

Davis, Cos H.
  Building bridges.

  1. Family—Religious life.   2. Parenting—
Religious aspects—Christianity.   3. Interpersonal
relations—Religious aspects—Christianity.
4. Children—Religious life.   I. Title.
BV4526.2.D38   1985   649'.1   84-17476
ISBN 0-8054-5659-7

This book is dedicated to Cos Nathan and Kristen Leigh, gifts from God. They have often been in my thoughts as I have written these pages, for they depend so much on me and their mother to build good bridges. We must not fail them.

CONTENTS

Bridges: The Idea

This book is about bridges and ways to build them. A bridge is simply a connecting link between two points—spanning a gulf, body of water, or chasm and allowing safe passage from one side to the other. Most bridges aren't too exciting, but many have served very useful purposes in our lives. Bridges may also be connecting links from one person to another. Think of how limited our relationships would be without bridges.

This book is also about the world's most important bridge-builders: parents. It is a book about parenting. This book will help you discover ways to build "bridges" to your child's future relationships with God and others.

Basics for Bridge Building

In order to rear healthy, positive children, parents must give priority to some basics for building bridges to future relationships.

First, *relationship is the most important thing in the world.* Relationship with God and others is the goal of life.

Parents must be able to teach children how to relate to God and to others in positive ways. Learning to live with honest appreciation of who God is, who he is, and who others are is the most important lesson a child can learn. The process of learning to relate to God and others is called bridge building.

Second, *home is the place.* Home offers the best possible opportunity for teaching about relationships. Through modeling families can demonstrate the importance of God and others. Home is essentially the classroom of life for the young child. God and others become important to the child if they are really important to you, the parent. Basic lessons of relationships—respect, forgiveness, honesty, tolerance, and kindness—can be taught in the home. There is no other setting with so much potential for building bridges to the future as the home.

Third, *parents are teachers.* Whether we like it or not, prepared or not, we become teachers when we become parents. Our relationships to God and each other are modeled and conveyed whether we want them to be or not. We are on display to our child! Values, fears, aspirations, and prejudices are taught through our daily routine of communicating. Yes, we are teachers, and the things we teach need to be the "stuff" bridges to future relationships are made of.

Fourth, *bridges to future relationships are needed.* As awesome as it may sound, your child's relationships to God and others, including his mate, are greatly affected by the home he grows up in and the way he learns to relate to others. While you will not determine his actual decisions to serve God, whom to marry, or whom to have as friends, you will set the emotional tone and background out of which he will make those decisions. If you can build some bridges, life will be much more positive and fulfilling for your child.

Fifth, *God is interested in the bridges we build.* Since life is God's gift to each of us, He is primarily concerned with its quality. He is concerned about His relationship to each of us and our relationship to each other. He has provided us with the perfect model for relationships in His Son, Jesus. Jesus' teaching in Matthew 22:36-40 emphasizes the priority of relationships that His life demonstrated. "Thou shalt love the Lord thy God with all thy heart, and with all thy soul, and with all thy mind. . . . Thou shalt love thy neighbour as thyself." (vv. 37-39). This is the essence of life—where bridges must be built.

God is interested in supplying the wisdom needed to build those bridges to Him and others. If we are willing to work hard and trust God, God will supply the wisdom needed. Parenting is the single most important assignment we will have in life. No one can do it as well as it should be done apart from God's help. Acknowledge your need and ask God to help you build those bridges. "If any of you lack wisdom, let him ask of God, . . . and it shall be given him" (Jas. 1:5).

A Bridge to God

The ultimate goal of life is for each child to know God and live in fellowship with Him. In order for her to do this you will need to build a bridge for her to understand God and relate to Him.

A child comes into the world with only a capacity to know God. The way in which a child thinks about or relates to a Higher Being will be determined by the way those closest to him relate to God. Most children grow up believing in God, but few grow up with a healthy understanding of and proper feelings toward God. Some children feel distrust for God, think He is spying on them, or feel that He's going to get them at the first wrong move they make. How did they get attitudes like that? On the other hand, there are young children whose parents have a growing, healthy respect for God. These children will grow up with a healthy attitude toward life and its Source. This attitude may be described as trust—absolutely essential to knowing God. (Heb. 11:6).

Why does one child learn to relate to God so readily while others have such difficulties believing that God really cares for them? Most likely it is because some parents build bridges while others unknowingly create a gulf between the child and God.

This brings us to a very important understanding: the role of parents in teaching children about God. Parents are the child's first impression of God. No one exists for the child beyond the parents for several months. In the early years the child is totally dependent on parents for all its needs. If these needs are met lovingly and the child is treated with care, he will develop a sense of trust toward his parent. The mother is often in the role of building early trust. The father should become involved as early as possible in the care of the child also in order to build an early emotional attachment with the child. The trust built in the early years will ultimately enable the child to transfer his trust from parent to God, assuming he has been taught that God can be trusted.

The basic attitude of trust so essential to relating properly to God is not magic. Trust is learned from you, the parent. The daily routine of meeting physical needs lovingly, listening to your child's concerns, and being excited about her developing abilities will build the bridge which can lead to God.

One more word on this subject. To build a good bridge to God will require that you know God in an intimate, personal, saving way. Otherwise, God will be distant and not very real to you or to your child. You need to exercise the joy of making God a part of all your life. This doesn't imply a sickening fanaticism where religious trappings are hung all over your house, and every word is pious. But it is a living, honest, growing relationship with God which will demonstrate who you believe God to be. You must trust the integrity of your relationship to God to convince your child that God is real and can be trusted.

A Bridge to Others

The other major bridge that you, as a parent, must construct is one which helps your child relate well to others. Children come with their own unique personalities; some are outgoing, and some are somewhat shy or withdrawn. These personality factors do not guarantee that the outgoing child will have no problems with relationships or that the shy child will never develop meaningful relationships with others. Good personal relationships demand more than being friendly or socially attractive. Having good relationships with others involves trust, respect, and the give and take of communication. All children—no matter what personalities they come with—need guidance in relationship with others.

The beginning place for your child is to help him develop a wholesome appreciation for himself. He must be guided to develop a loving appreciation for who he is—a good self-concept. This is the foundation for the bridge to others, and to God. Only as he values himself can he value others.

There are two possibilities of human relationships in your child's future: friends and a marriage partner. The ability to make friends and to be a friend is a sign of growth. It involves the ability to care for others without using them, to share mutual concerns, and to enjoy the company of another person. Children who are taught that they are truly cared for and respected do not find such attitudes difficult to express toward others. Children reared in an atmosphere where parents relate positively to each other and to others are equipped with understanding and skills which will lead to good personal relationships. Bridges are being built for them.

The kind of marriage partner a child later chooses (if she chooses to marry) and how she relates to them is also influenced by you, the parent. From her early days she has been eyewitness to your respect (or lack of respect) for each other as persons, to the way you attack each other or your problems, and your tenderness with each other. In all of this, a child makes interpretations of what a husband, wife, and family are. It might surprise you to think of ways your father or mother have unconsciously influenced your decision to marry the kind of person you have married.

As you model marriage relationships before your child, you are making it easier or more difficult for him to have an honest, growing relationship with that husband or wife who is in their future. The following pages will help you to know how to build a bridge rather than create a gulf.

To Think About

Discuss with your spouse the idea that parenting is a task of building bridges to future relationships for your child.

PART 1
PARENTS/BRIDGE BUILDERS

1
Now's the Time for Building Bridges

Close to the rural area where I grew up is a small, two-lane bridge I drive across every time I visit my parents. This bridge stands today, as it has for over sixty years, as a physical legacy of my grandfather who helped build the bridge. Almost every time I cross the bridge, I recall things my father told me about who my grandfather was, how he died, and what he was like.

While I never saw or knew my grandfather, I know that he and the other builders were interested in quality work —a bridge that would last. Much attention was given to laying a good foundation to support the weight of the superstructure and its traffic. Every time I drive across the bridge, I trust my life and that of my wife and children to the integrity and strength of the bridge's foundation.

In life, just as in bridges, houses, or any other structure, the foundation is the most critical consideration. No matter how beautiful the exterior may look, a structure's endurance is dependent on the foundation. A child's life is no different. We assume that people who have built bridges and other structures know how to build good foundations, and we trust our life and those of our loved ones to these builders. Yet we rarely give thought to the importance of foundations for our young child's life. Jesus' illustration of two builders in the closing of the Sermon on the Mount in Matthew 7:24-27 should remind us that laying foundations for life is serious business!

We should also be aware that the time we have to build foundations is very brief. The most critical time is the first six years of life. Parents of young children or those considering having children need to realize the critical importance of the first six years of life in building bridges to the future.

Foundations for Living

Many experts in the field of childhood education contend that the first six years of life are the most critical in the development of the personality of the individual. While other stages are important, the experiences of these early years seem to have more effect on the development of one's self-concept and personality. The human being experiences radical changes physically and intellectually during these first six years. The child advances from an almost totally dependent state at birth to a person who is quite developed in physical abilities by age six. Intellectually, the child learns more in these six years than any other six years in life. Never again will learning be so rapid.

Erik Erikson[1] has aided parents tremendously by identifying some of the major learning tasks for young children. The parents' role is highly significant in helping their child proceed from one stage to the next. Erikson has identified these stages as "psycho-social" tasks. The following paragraphs identify these stages and the way they relate to you, the parent.

Trust

The first task in developing a sense of importance and worth as a person is the child's development of trust in parents. This sense of emotional well-being is essential if the new life is to grow into a loving, responsible individual. The baby develops trust when parents are positive that they want the child and are attentive to physical needs for food, warmth, diaper changes, and being held lovingly, talked to, and played with.

Underlying the development of trust in the young child is the commitment of the parents to give what the child needs physically and emotionally. Because of the needs in early infancy, the young child must receive a great deal of time and energy from both parents. The burden for much of the early development of the young child rests with the loving care of the mother. Studies are showing, however, that the father can also be of great help in the proper development of the personality of the young child. He needs to make himself available to assist the mother in whatever way possible. Not only will this help the father in developing his relationship to his child but will be of great benefit in the event the mother becomes ill and cannot do as much for the child.

Christian parents should realize that the development of trust in them by their child is a continuing need. It does not just happen, overnight. A child never outgrows his need for trust. Children need a continuing relationship where they can trust parents to meet their needs and always do what is best for them. The need for trust begins at birth but continues throughout life.

Another important aspect of trust needs to be understood by parents. The trust a child develops in parents is basic or foundational to the child's trust in God. If, for example, your child can trust you he can believe that God exists and that God loves and cares for him. Later, the bridge to faith you have built can be used to relate to God and others in a healthy and useful way.

Some people have no trust. They are miserable, skeptical about life, and basically negative about everything. If they believe in God, they do not really feel that He loves them personally. How do people come to be so miserable and unhappy? It would be a good guess to say that they never developed a proper sense of trust when they were young. Somehow they never felt they were really loved and could trust the parents who brought them into the world. Once mistrust has become a settled outlook on life, such people interpret all of life from this perspective. Though they wish things could be different, they are so emotionally bound to the teaching of their early years that to escape seems almost impossible.

Autonomy

God has planned that physical and intellectual growth in the child push him to accomplish important tasks. Once your child feels she can trust you, she can build on that trust to develop a sense of autonomy or independence. You have seen her developing such progressive physical skills as turning over, sitting up, scooting, crawling, pulling up to stand, and standing alone. Do you know what is happening? Your child is preparing to accomplish another milestone. She is preparing to take her first step!

At about the time a child reaches the stage of walking, she will be attempting to become more and more independent. Newly developed skills allow more freedom from adults and allow more exploration than before. As the child discovers the world around her, she will discover more and more about herself. She will begin to realize that she is a person apart from her parents. She is developing a self-identity. She can do more things for herself and should be allowed to do what she can do.

You will likely sense that your child has changed a great deal emotionally as well as physically. These months can be stormy and frustrating for child and parents. Your once calm and placid baby may exhibit a "temper" which you thought was impossible for your "little angel." Likely, she has attempted to do something which is beyond her ability and has become frustrated. Her reaction is to cry. Or perhaps you have restrained your child from an activity you thought would be dangerous, such as climbing up and standing on top of a table. (Yes, she may really try it). Her reaction may be rage.

As a parent you must determine your strategy on the basis of what this period is all about for your child. She has not determined in her mind to personally wreck your house and kill herself in the process. No, she is being pushed from within to develop a sense of autonomy. If you keep this need in mind, you can cope more lovingly and constructively with the tantrums and the constant activity which may be part of your life.

Your role in the development of your child's independence should be to recognize it as normal, want it for your child, and allow its expression within safe limits. Practically, this means making your home child proof by putting up breakable objects, and household cleaners, and keeping dangerous objects and furniture with sharp corners out of the way. You will also want to cover electrical receptacles with safety covers and check to see if any of your household plants are poisonous. You will be surprised to find that many such plants are poisonous. Be sure. While you cannot protect your child from everything, and should not try to, you should try to eliminate potentially dangerous situations.

Bumps and bruises will be part of your child's life for a while and should be expected. Your child cannot make judgments about what will be harmful. You must do that.

However, parents are sometimes so concerned about protecting their child from getting hurt that they stifle the need to explore and learn. While proper toys for this age should be bought, it should also be remembered that such items as pots and pans and books can be explored as part of this growing process.

Perhaps the most important rule to remember is: allow your child to do what she can for herself. As you observe her abilities and what she can do, you will be more aware of when to "keep hands off." Do not take her growing independence as a sign she does not need you. She still needs you in many ways. What she needs most is your loving understanding and the freedom and encouragement to do what she can for herself.

Initiative

Beginning at about age three and continuing through age five, your child will be attempting to deal with the task Erikson calls initiative. For your child, this is basically developing ideas of his own and his own way to do things. He becomes an initiator because of his new ideas. He is more noticeably deliberate in the way he attacks a problem. He is more prone to try to "figure it out" than he once was. You can observe this readily by watching your child work an appropriate puzzle. He will generally move a piece around until it fits properly in its place.

Of course, your child is still dealing with trust and autonomy while focusing more clearly on initiative. You should always keep in mind that trust and autonomy are essential to initiative. Your child will still need to feel that sense of personal security and independence which have freed him to learn about you, his world and himself.

It is during this developmental stage of initiative that conscience begins to develop. Your child seems to become concerned with the "rightness and wrongness" of his actions. He is particularly vulnerable to feelings of guilt and lack of personal worth. Your major task is to take care not to make unimportant incidents, such as spills or crayon markings, a moral issue. Give more attentions to a positive relationship to your child. Give sincere praise for his accomplishments, encourage him, and help him feel good about himself. If he feels good about himself, he will be released to attempt new things and accomplish new heights in his personal development. If you help him feel good about himself, you will notice that he will attempt to correct unacceptable behavior in order to please you.

The tasks of trust, autonomy, and initiative are bridges for a healthy, growing person to experience the best in relationships with others and with God. Obviously, a great deal of this ability to relate well to man and God is provided in the bridges built by parents in the early years of their child's life. During these early years, basic attitudes toward life and the all-important feeling about self are established. While a person's attitudes and feelings are not set in concrete, they can only be altered later with great effort.

It is important to understand that you, the parent, are the primary teacher of attitudes and feelings which help your child to determine his own personal worth. Future relationships with others and God will be helped or hindered by the way you have prepared your child for life during these early years. One educator put it this way: "Childhood is the time to establish a foundation of meaning upon which commitment can be built."[2]

As parents, God has entrusted to you a great gift—a child. To you and you alone He has given the privileges of personal growth and responsibility involved in being a parent. You cannot transfer your parenting responsibility to grandparents, schools, church, or anyone else. God has given you the privilege of working with Him to help finish this unfinished creation.

The greatest work in the world is that of growing loving, trusting persons within the family. Look again at the child God has given you. Now is the time to work! Now is the time for building bridges to the future.

To Think About

1. Why are the early years so critical in building bridges in the child's life?

2. Why are trust, autonomy, and initiative important as foundations for living?

2
Who Am I?

This book is about parents building bridges for their young child to future relationships with others and with God. You are reading this because you are interested in helping your child have positive relationships. You were once a child. Parents and others have influenced the attitudes and feelings you have brought to adulthood and to your parenting task. You have been aided or hindered by your own parents by the bridges or barriers to relationships they have built in your life.

To do your best possible job as a parent, you need to look for some answers to the question, Who am I?" You are a person with a past which will influence your attitude toward yourself, others, and God. The whole issue in knowing who you are and how this relates to parenting is well-stated in these words:

The most important thing adults can do to help build a healthy self-image in a child is to possess a positive self-image of their own. Far too many scars are transmitted to children as parents express their own deep-seated frustrations, ambitions and resentments.[3]

Parents each bring a positive self-image or emotional scars to their bridge-building task. All persons are the sum total of their experiences and interpretations of those experiences. There is nothing "magical" about having a child which will make us a better or different person.

Having a child often challenges parents to look at the possibility of change. Change is possible. But if the need for change is ever realized, it must be felt on the basis of what parents know themselves to be now.

Why It's Important to Know Who You Are

Parents teach their children basically two kinds of truth: objective and subjective—facts and feelings. While teaching correct factual information is important, the feelings parents teach are even more influential. Children can learn factual information through many sources, but feelings of self-worth and love are taught primarily through relationship with parents. It is likely that the relationship you have with your child will overpower whatever factual knowledge your child might have. Being told he is loved never takes the place of being shown. How good it is to be shown *and* told!

You are building your child's life for future relationships. You are laying those foundations primarily through who you are and your relationship to your child. You will essentially teach your child from the overflow of your life. Your sense of self-worth, values, and goals will be the resources from which your child will learn. You cannot separate who you are from the way you approach your role as a parent.

There are two Scripture references which will help you to see that all of life proceeds from attitudes deep within. As you read these passages remember that the word *heart* is used to designate that which is at the core of one's being. In the "heart" reside the values, aspirations, and commitments of one's outward life.

> Keep thy heart with all diligence; for out of it are the issues of life (Prov. 4:23).
>
> A good man out of the good treasure of his heart bringeth forth that which is good; and an evil man out of the evil treasure of his heart bringeth forth that which is evil: for of the abundance of the heart his mouth speaketh (Luke 6:45).

At the "heart of your life the real you lives." How you feel about yourself, about possessions, about God, about others will determine how you live.

Although adults differ from their parents in many ways, it is amazing to notice the similarity of values and attitudes that have remained through the years. Such values and attitudes are formed early in life and tend to control much of what we do as adults. The arresting point of all of this is that we are developing a person's outlook on life through the values and attitudes we model at home.

In my kitchen in a conspicious place hangs a plaque with these haunting words:

> If a child lives with criticism, he learns to condemn.

If a child lives with hostility, he learns to fight.
If a child lives with ridicule, he learns to be shy.
If a child lives with shame, he learns to feel guilty.
If a child lives with tolerance, he learns to be patient.
If a child lives with encouragement, he learns confidence.
If a child lives with praise, he learns to appreciate.
If a child lives with fairness, he learns justice.
If a child lives with security, he learns to have faith.
If a child lives with approval, he learns to like himself.
If a child lives with acceptance, and friendship, he learns
  to find love in the world.

You cannot teach what you are not anymore than you can lead someone where you have never been. But don't be discouraged! If you need to make some changes, God's grace is sufficient! First, you must get to know yourself, know what needs to be changed to make you the parent you need to be, and make a real commitment to change.

Getting to Know Yourself

Some people spend most or perhaps all of their life not really knowing who they are. One reason for this is fear. Perhaps they are afraid to ask too many honest questions. Sometimes the answers are painful. But the alternative is even more painful and tragic. They never get to know why they have the values, attitudes, or goals they do. Having never discovered some of the illogical reasons they feel the way they do, they cannot deal with problems they have.

The brief exercise which follows is designed to help you discover attitudes, goals, and values you have now and to make a decision about the person you really want to be for God, yourself, your mate, and your child. Such a decision may mean giving up some of your present attitudes, goals, and values. Look at the way you feel about certain areas in your life.

Mom and Dad

Recall your days at home with Mom and Dad. How do you really, honestly feel about your parents? Did you feel wanted? Loved? What do you like most about your dad? What do you like least about him? What do you like most about your mom? What do you like least about her? What do you want your family to have that you had at home? What you do not want in your family that you had in your home? Did one parent seem to be more dominant than the other? How would you describe your parents' relationship? What are some attitudes, values, or goals which have been deeply influenced by your experience at home?

Take some time to think through your answers. Be as honest as you can be. Jot down significant experiences which you think have had a major influence on who you are today.

Brothers and Sisters

What are the names of brothers or sisters? Which are older? Which are younger? Did you experience difficulty in being the oldest, middle, or youngest in the family? Was there a sense of rivalry with any brother or sister? Was one brother or sister closer than others? Why do you think this was so? How do you feel about your brothers or sisters today? Are you close to them? Do you have trouble with them? Are you friends? How do you feel your brothers or sisters have influenced who you are?

Again, take time to honestly answer these questions. Write down significant events which have influenced you.

Only Child

Perhaps you were an only child. How do you feel having no brothers or sisters influenced who you are? What were the advantages? Disadvantages?

Other Relatives

Did any relatives such as grandparents live in your home? Did you live in their home? How did you feel about this arrangement? Did your parents and grandparents get along well?

Did a relative show favoritism toward you or a brother or sister? Were there any experiences with grandparents or other relatives, positive or negative, which have had a real impact on your life?

Tragedies

Were there some personal tragedies in your childhood which may have had an impact on the way you look at life? Was there a death of a parent or sibling? If so, how have you dealt with that? Are you resentful, angry, or reconciled and at peace about the death? Did your parents divorce? If so, how did you feel about that? Did you face some personal physical tragedy as a child, such as serious burns, a crippling accident, or a crippling childhood disease? Were you physically or emotionally abused as a child?

Investigate to see how you have handled tragedies in your life. Is there any lasting effect or attitude related to the tragedy? What emotional scars or strengths will you bring to your parenting task?

Religious Training

To what degree did your parents guide your religious development? What specific activities, such as Bible stories, prayer, or church attendance, did they use to guide you? Was religion enjoyable most of the time? What role did your parents play in your conversion? Were they a real help or a hindrance?

What do you feel about God on the basis of what your parents taught you? What will you attempt to change or keep in religious training for your children?

Communication

How would you describe communication between you and your parents when you were a child? What were some good experiences? What were some communication problems your family had? How have you decided to be different as a parent?

Discipline

Were you allowed to do whatever you wished without restrictions? Do you feel your parents were too strict, too lenient, or moderate? What methods of discipline and encouragement did they use? Were they fair? Consistent? Did they often encourage you? Did they criticize you? Did they tend to deal more with the wrong action or with your personality?

How do you feel your homelife has equipped you as a parent in the area of discipline?

Sex Education

How did you grow up feeling about your body and its functions? What did your mom and dad do to make you feel good that you were you? Did they talk with you about your body and sexual organs? Did they explain their use and proper respect for them?

Where and from whom did you get your basic information and attitudes about sex? What attitudes do you want to communicate about sex to your child?

Financial Education

You have brought attitudes about money and possessions to your marriage and your child-rearing responsibility. What, in your opinion, is the purpose of money and possessions? Where did you get your ideas about money and possessions? How do you really feel about money? Are material possessions really important to you?

Were your parents rich, poor, middle-class? What were their attitudes about possessions? Do you see any of their influence in your attitudes? If so, what? How did your parents manage their money? What were the results?

How do you respond to the statement in 1 Timothy

6:10? "The love of money is the root of all evil". How important is money and what it can do for you?

To Think About

This practical exercise will help you to see how you have been influenced for good or bad by others in your choice of values for living. List the values by which you live. Put them in priority order. A good way to begin is simply to ask: "What is most important to me right now?" Your list may include such things as your relationships to God, your spouse, child, and possessions. Whatever you do, be honest with yourself.

How do these values reflect your rearing? What do you really want for your life?

After both husband and wife have completed the practical exercise above, spend at least one hour talking about what's important to each of you, why it is important, and what each of you would like to change in yourself.

3
Counting the Cost

Most couples have little difficulty in conceiving a child. But the ability to have a child does not insure that you are ready for the experience of parenthood or that you will be good parents. There are a great number of real changes a couple must be willing to make in their life-style when they decide to have a child.

In his book *Is There a Family in the House?*, Kenneth Chafin makes the following observations:

> No activity in which couples participate requires a larger investment or brings a larger return than parenting. . . . bringing "quality" to parenting is the most important task confronting our society today. . . . Parenting is not some intuitive skill which you either have or don't have. Babies are born but parenting skills are developed.[4]

To become a good parent involves a sizable investment. You will need an understanding of some of the costs involved and your willingness to pay them. This chapter will focus on some of those costs. You will be challenged to look at some of your personal and family goals and to ask if there is room for a child in your life.

What Are Your Priorities?

To rear healthy children who are capable of responding adequately to God and others requires that your child receive an adequate amount of your time and energy. Each of us has only twenty-four hours in each day. The way we spend our time says something about our priorities. Hard decisions must be made about whether you are ready to have a child. If you already have a child, you need to consider whether or not he is getting what he needs from you.

Many times persons are faced with making decisions about "good" things in their lives. Is it possible that you need to give up something "good" in order to give proper attention to your child? One of the real dangers facing Christians today is too much involvement in the "good" so that no time and energy are left for the "best" in life.

The best things in life have to do with relationships—to God, to spouse, to children, and to others. Even "good" things become bad when persons allow them to take the place of the best.

Whether you already have a child or are considering having one, you would do well to look at some of your goals in the following areas.

Your Marriage

Is your marriage on trial, or are both of you committed to make it work no matter what? Obviously, if you are tentative about your commitment to each other you are not ready to complicate your life with a child. A child is not an easy solution to an uncertain or troubled marriage. Take time to get to know each other (a couple of years, at least) and feel comfortable with who you are as a couple.

Before having a child, your major priority should be to establish a good marriage through the blending of your personalities. For some, this period of adjustment may take longer than for others because of different backgrounds, shorter engagements, or other aspects. However long it takes, take the time to feel comfortable about the direction of your marriage and your mutual goals. Because of various considerations, my wife and I waited six years before having our first child. And we're glad we did. The important thing is for both of you to be ready for another member of the family.

Educational Goals

Do you or your spouse have educational goals which will make being a parent more difficult? While education is important, your child's well-being in the early years should not be sacrificed for schooling. If you feel that more education is a must right now, perhaps deciding to wait on having children is best for your family. If you have a child and decide to forego more education for a few years, your child should not be the victim of the frustration you may face because of your decision. Whatever decision you make, do it with a willingness to pay the price for your decision.

Sometimes young couples have a child before the husband has completed his education, and the wife works while he finishes school. While the father's schooling may mean a better family financial situation later, the child may be paying a tremendous price in her early, formative years. Great care needs to be taken in making decisions about the alternatives in situations such as this.

Finances

When my wife and I were thinking about having our first child, an older friend advised me: "You'll never have enough money to have a child. You may as well go ahead and have one." While there is some truth in the idea that you may never have "enough" money to rear children, there should be enough financial stability to provide what the family needs without both marriage partners feeling forced to work. It is often wise for partners to work and save for a few years before deciding to have children. That way you can buy many of the basic things needed for the household before the expenses of rearing a child come along.

Some couples decide that the wife will quit work and take care of the young child until the child goes to school. While the couple may have less money to spend they will have fewer taxes, less work-related expenses, and less hassle about the extra demands the child has brought upon them. Many couples decide to "survive" for a few years, and many times the child is the beneficiary of such a decision.

Care needs to be given in the financial decisions you

make because the child may end up paying part of the bill. You may need to alter your wishes and not get caught in a financial trap which forces you to do something you may not really want to do. For instance, I have known of situations where couples were working. They thought they needed another car. They couldn't afford it if the wife didn't work. So they bought the car, and she was trapped in a job to pay for the car she was driving to work!

Freedom

Couples without children have much more personal freedom than those who have children. There are less demands on their time and energy. They have no worries or anxieties about anyone but themselves. Couples without children have a comparatively free and simple life!

The decision to have children is a decision to give up much of your freedom. You become responsible for another person who is completely dependent on you. Lack of time, energy, and money after having a child may curtail many of your activities. You will not have the same freedom to go or spend as you once did. Even if you do have the money, you may not have the energy to make the effort. This may sound like an exaggeration but these strong statements are to help you realize that there will be a drastic change in your life-style once a child has arrived.

Some couples see the loss of freedom as a reason not to have children. Personally, I have found the benefits of growing with my children to be far greater than the personal freedom I had before Nathan and Kristen were born.

But you and your spouse are the ones who must decide. If you decide to have children, you should be able to do so with a deliberate choice for the benefits of parenthood over those of personal freedom.

Giving Your Child the Best

Many parents enter upon the adventure of parenthood with the idea that they want their child to "have the best." What is meant by "the best" is probably different for almost every couple. In fact, many have only vague feelings about this "best" they have never defined. They have never spent the energy to think about what "the best" really is.

Some parents define "the best" as having what advertisers and society consider "the best": "the best" house, clothes, food, car, toys, schools, and so forth. What's wrong with this? Nothing, except that parents sometimes think that these things constitute "the best" and think they have fulfilled their parental duties by providing them. In our materialistic society it is often easy for a Christian parent to fall into this trap. We must keep our focus about what "the best" is for our child and allow no substitutes, no matter how good they may seem to be.

In rearing our children we are confronted with a society which continually puts an emphasis on having and acquiring things. This philosophy of life says, "A person's riches consist of the things he possesses." Jesus' caution regarding things is: "Take heed, and beware of covetousness: for a man's life consisteth not in the abundance of the things which he possesseth" (Luke 12:15).

For the Christian parent, "the best" must be defined in biblical terms of relationship with God and other persons. Practically, this means focusing your attention on those things which relate to the personhood of your child. It means giving your child "the best" person you can be as a parent. What are some practical aspects of giving your child "the best" person you can be?

Spiritually

As parents, we should be committed to God and His purpose for our lives. Outer expressions of inner spiritual life such as Bible reading and prayer should produce growth and spiritual understanding. Time needs to be given to spiritual development which means making reading Scripture and devotional materials and prayer a priority.

You will teach your child through who you are more than through what you say. Haim Ginott was correct when he said, "character traits cannot be transmitted by words but must be demonstrated."[5]

Consider the following question as you think about the implications of your spiritual life to your child: "If your child grows up to be like you, what kind of a person will he be?"

Quality Time

The important issue regarding time spent with your child seems to be quality rather than quantity. It is conceivable that a woman who is unhappy with staying at home might be better off at work.

Whatever your decision about both parents working, strong consideration needs to be given to spending quality time with your child. Time should be scheduled each day with no interruptions allowed for telephone calls, washing dinner dishes, or other chores. Both parents need to make time to play with and enjoy their child, sing to her, talk to her. Play games with your child while bathing or dressing her. You will experience her delight with you, and you will enjoy being with your child and watching her develop.

The mother who stays home has a real advantage for making almost any routine a special time for her child. Talking with or singing to your child can make for many enjoyable moments. But the advantage is a real one only if the mother is happy with her situation and will utilize the additional opportunities she has to relate positively to her child.

To Think About

The following exercise is designed to help you count the cost of having a child.

1. List your personal goals, in such areas as education, financial, or travel. Beside each item state how you think having a child may alter your goals.
2. Research the financial costs of having a baby. Check with your physician and the local hospital. Verify how much of the bill your insurance will pay.
3. Talk with two other Christian couples about the

types of adjustments they are facing because of a child. Don't forget to ask them about the joys of parenthood also.

4. List any personal changes you will need to make to give your child "the best" possible you.
Husband:
Wife:

PART 2
BLUEPRINT FOR BUILDING BRIDGES

4
The Gift

By now it should be obvious that good parents have highly positive attitudes about themselves and their children. While certain parenting skills must be learned, Christian parenting is marked primarily by the unmistakable certainty that a child is a gift from God. Flowing from this understanding is a commitment to be a good steward of the child (gift) God has given.

To help you as parents explore the concept of the child as a gift, here are three basic questions: (1) Where do children come from? (2) Why does God give us children? (3) What do we do with a gift?

Where Do Children Come From?

This seems to be a simple question to answer, and it is. But there is overwhelming profundity in the simplicity of the answer.

Before you get to the biblical answer to this question, consider some possible options.

Option one: A child is only the product of a normal sexual function. Those who think this way relish the miracle "they have created" by themselves. There is no first cause, no recognition of the Creator. While parents may accept total responsibility to be good parents, a very vital aspect of parenting is missing: the privilege of consciously working with God to mold this new life.

Option two: A child is an accident. For some couples a child is unplanned. Nevertheless, conception takes place, and the child is born. Parents who complain about "the accident" obviously do not take responsibility for their sexual conduct. Even while birth control measures are used, a possibility for conception still remains. No birth control method is 100 percent "safe" with all couples. While the child is unplanned, he does not have to be unwanted. Once the pregnancy is certain, both partners need to fully accept their actions and make the child feel wanted.

Option three: A child is a gift of God. While accepting responsibility for sexual intercourse, partners should also recognize that the ability to have children from their union is a gift from God. Christian couples should allow scriptural attitudes and concepts to dictate their thinking about children.

Consider the following biblical concepts as you think about what a child means to you.

The ability to procreate children is a blessing from God. Genesis 1:28 says of Adam and Eve. "God blessed them, and God said unto them, Be fruitful, and multiply, and replenish the earth, and subdue it." God blessed Adam and Eve, and mankind, with the ability to reproduce our own kind. This sexual function is not a cosmic accident, but it is in God's plan for human happiness and God's purposes. To personalize this a bit more, your ability to conceive a child is a gift from God to you!

Psalm 127:3 is just one of many references to the fact that a child is a gift from God: "Lo, children are an heritage from the Lord: and the fruit of the womb is his reward."

The Old Testament is filled with the idea that a child is a gift from God. Out of this rich background, Christians should approach the experience of parenting with a special sense of wonder, awe, and gratitude for the gift of a child.

Few cultures have valued children as much as that of the Hebrews. In Old Testament times a man's true wealth and strength were often measured in terms of his children —particularly the number of them. Psalm 127:4-5 gives an intriguing view of what children are to a family. "As arrows are in the hand of a mighty man; so are children of the youth. Happy is the man that hath his quiver full of them."

While we may conclude that we ought to limit the number of children we have because of physical, economic, or other reasons, we must agree that our true wealth is in our children. Just ask any grandparent!

Some time ago Nathan asked me, "Daddy, are we rich?" Kristen overheard the question and, like Nathan, was awaiting the verdict. While I tried to assure them that we had what we needed, I also wanted to assure them of what is most valuable to our family. I made a reply something like this: "We don't have lots of money, but we're rich. Know why? Because your mother and I have Nathan and Kristen, and we're rich!" What a delightful insight: how reassuring for my children that they are gifts!

An even deeper beauty of this encounter was seen at a later time when we were again talking about possessions, and Kristen chimed, "Daddy, we're rich aren't we? Know why? Cause you've got me and Nathan." My deepest aspirations as a father were affirmed when that beautiful little girl said those words. Something of inestimatable value had been communicated to her. She could understand and treasure the thought of her great worth to the most important people in her life.

Perhaps the greatest insight you will have concerning your child is the one so basic to all that you must do for him: your child is a gift from God. God made him and placed him in your care.

Why Children?

Several years ago a book was published with the title *Why God Gave Children Parents*. That fine work emphasized the responsibilities of parents toward their children and the benefits they could be to their children. But have you ever thought about why God gives parents children? Certainly every child is a gift because of the potential of his life. But this gift can enhance the lives of the people to whom the child is given: his parents. Here are some personal insights about why God gave me children. Perhaps these ideas will be helpful to you.

To Enhance Our Relationship with God

While parents are teachers, they are to be learners also. There are many times when God uses children to teach parents about Him and how He cares for people. It is not by coincidence that Jesus used family terms to describe the believer's relationship to God. He tells us to speak to God in the warm and intimate term of "Our Father." We are brothers and sisters of the family of "Our Father." We are His children.

It is through the gift of a child that parents often learn the more intimate things about their relationship to their Heavenly Father. It is how they learn the meaning of complete trust and abandonment. Children trust their parents to meet every need of their lives. They do not worry about the necessities of life. Why should they when they have parents who really love them? Does this say anything about the need for complete trust and abandonment to God in the parents' lives? If you as a parent can love your child so deeply that you will do everything in your power to give him what he needs, how much greater is God's love and how much more will He do for His children! Consider what Jesus is saying about trust in these words in Matthew 7:9-11:

What man is there of you, whom if his son ask for bread, will he give him a stone? Or if he ask a fish, will he give him a serpent? If ye then, being evil, know how to give good gifts unto your children, how much more shall your Father which is in heaven give good things to them that ask him?

The obvious conclusion from this passage is that persons who call the perfect and holy God "Father" can trust Him with every need and detail of their lives. Children can help parents learn to trust.

To Renew Our Wonder About the Miracle of Life

There is the tendency in each of us to forget that life itself is a miracle. Work and school do not necessarily focus on the essentials of life. They do not readily draw a person's attention to God and to the miracle of life.

What better way to stir gratitude or to evoke wonder than with a baby! A newborn infant is "freshest" from heaven, and nothing so renews our sense of awe and wonder about life. There is something intensely spiritual and sacred about the birth of a child that should move us to thanksgiving and praise.

With the birth of a child we are moved to acknowledge again that God is the loving Source of life.

To Renew Our Hope

As I write, there is trouble all over our world. Wars or military action of some kind are raging in at least forty different places on the earth. The threat of nuclear war is very real. The future does not look very bright.

Some well-meaning friends or relatives may advise you not to have children in such troubled times. Certainly a person has to be aware of the world around him when he makes such decisions. While having children is your choice, you should not listen only to "doomsday" talk.

God allows us to have children to improve the world, to

offer hope to humanity. For the Christian, having children and rearing them to serve the Lord offers a ray of hope for the world. If God had considered only the bad social, political, and economic conditions, He would never have allowed Jesus to have been born when He was!

There is a sense in which having children is an act of ministry for the Christian. The Christian couple who seeks God's guidance about having and rearing children will likely bring to the world a child who can make a great contribution for good.

The good a child can do once he matures is what this book is all about. It is about a positive relationship with God and others. It is about hope. It is about parents bringing hope to the world through healthy children. A very wise man once wrote of this hope the world so desperately needs. He said that every child comes with a reminder that God is not yet discouraged of man.

What Do You Do with a Gift?

This discussion of the child as a gift would not be complete without some thought being given to what to do with that "gift." Consider, if you will, what you should do with any gift.

Receive the Gift Gratefully

A gift is exactly that: a gift. The dictionary defines gift as something given or bestowed. It is not earned but given and should be received with that in mind. A gift is an expression or reminder of the giver's care for the receiver. A gift should be received with gratitude toward the giver.

When God gives a couple the unparalleled gift of a child, the response should be one of thankfulness and worship. Other than one's personal relationship to God and to one's mate, nothing can rival the value of a child. Celebration, thanksgiving, and joy are in order!

Remember the Giver

In every room in my house there are tangible reminders (gifts) of my contact with people over the years. Some of those gifts have special importance to me because they remind me of significant people in my life. A picture over the table, a flower arrangement, a radio, a candleholder, an oil lamp—all these and many more evoke memories of different times and meaningful relationships. With fondness I remember the giver.

My children, Nathan and Kristen, are gifts from God. They are also reminders of a relationship my wife and I have with each other and with God. Through our physical union we have been the recipients of the gift of children. We must attempt to live in constant recognition of that fact.

One way to demonstrate your recognition that God is the Giver of your child is to privately and publicly acknowledge it. Personally acknowledge God's goodness to your home through your conversation with each other and your prayers of thanksgiving. Publicly acknowledge His goodness through a dedication service for you and your child. In this way you can show other believers what God has given you.

Be a Good Steward

First Corinthians 4:2 is a statement worthy of consideration at this point, "It is required of stewards that one be found trustworthy" (NASB). The idea of this statement is that one who is entrusted with a gift should be responsible for it. Accepting responsibility for the physical, emotional, intellectual, and spiritual needs of my child is where responsible parenting begins. Some gifts need no further attention than placing them in an important place and giving them an occasional dusting. Not so with a child-gift! Children are not finished products by any means. They will need almost constant attention and care. You no longer belong to just yourself and your mate. You belong to a child and your child belongs to you.

Enjoy Your Gift

While children are an unmatched responsibility they are also a great joy. Parents should not lose or neglect this perspective. Watching them grow and develop brings pleasure. Children keep excitement in life. The things they say and do will be your gifts to treasure through the years. Take pleasure in them. Enjoy them, play with them, grow with them. You will discover new depths of feelings you are now unaware of as you experience your children. You will also notice a growing sense of joy in being with them. Parenting has a great number of joys yet for you to discover. I hope you find every one of them.

To Think About

1. How do you think a parent who sees his child as a gift is different from one who does not see his child in this way?

2. How will treating a child as a gift help to build bridges to his relationship to God and others?

5

Love—the Most Necessary Thing

The word *love* is very tricky. It has so many different meanings in society that you cannot assume the other person knows what you mean when you use it. Part of this confusion is due to the communication problems people can have with almost any word. There is not always a common understanding of the intent or meaning of a word by both the user and the hearer.

Perhaps it would help to clearly differentiate the basic kinds of love. The New Testament uses a unique word to describe God's love. The word used in John 3:16 for love is *agape.* The word describes God's choice to do only good for persons—to work in their lives only for those things that will help them to be better. His love is sacrificial and generous. It puts human good before anything else!

Another type of love is the kind of love friends would have for each other. This is a love one can have for a person of the same or the other sex without violating marital relationships or other biblical guidelines.

Obviously, the other type of love is sexual love. This is a love of a unique relationship a couple should have.

While it has dimensions of the other types of love, it is a love reserved exclusively for one's marriage partner.

Which of the three types of love described above should most nearly identify the love parents have for their children? I will discuss parental love in some detail later.

Another point of confusion about love is that some identify it as a feeling—an emotion. While love has feelings attached to it, it is much more than a feeling. For example, if love were an emotion or feeling, I could only love when I felt like it. The times I felt negative emotions would be times when I could not love. Anger, a legitimate emotion, would not be permissible at all. The truth is, I can be angry with my child and love him at the same time. Love must control my anger in a constructive way.

Another area of concern for most young parents is the conflict between what the child wants and what her parents think is best for her in a particular situation. Loving a child does not mean giving her what she wants; it is always giving her what is best for her. Often parents are emotionally manipulated by their child to go against their better judgment and give in to her. If the tears and tantrum had not influenced the decision, they would have done something entirely different. In situations such as this parents often react negatively and punitively toward the child rather than standing their ground and letting the child "cry it out."

What is Parent Love?

A parent's love for a child is similar to God's love for persons. Parental love is action. Parental love considers how it can best meet its responsibility to the child (gift) God has given. Parental love is taking parental stewardship seriously by acting in the best interest of the child. It is speaking and doing with the good of the child as its goal. Parental actions may include compliments or correction, playing and praying, challenging, guiding, encouraging, and listening. Parents may experience a wide variety of emotions such as anger and joy, excitement and anxiety as they love their child. Love will help these emotions to serve what is best for your child because love is doing what is best for your child.

Love Is Meeting Needs

Part of the problem in being human is that parents cannot always determine what is best for their children. Perhaps you need to start with some of his or her basic needs. What are they and how do they spell *love* for your child?

Love is communicated many ways to the young child, but it always results in two things: (1) her needs are met; and (2) her sense of personal worth is enhanced. Your child's needs fall basically into the following categories: physical, social, intellectual, emotional, and spiritual. Specific needs often overlap in these areas. For example, feeding your child obviously meets her physical need but also communicates an important message in other need areas such as social and emotional. Do not forget that a child is a whole person and will need nurturing in areas that are not necessarily physical.

You can use the child's emotional needs as a basis for

showing that when these needs are met other needs are met and vice versa. There are seven basic needs that are part of being loved. Consequently, when these needs are met your child feels loved.

Self-Esteem

Some people who have worked with and studied young children for years believe that building a healthy self-respect is the best thing parents can do for their children. I am among the group that puts self-esteem at the top of the list. Although the following chapter is devoted to this subject, it is well to give self-image some attention at this point.

Self-esteem refers to the way a person feels about herself. She can have a low self-esteem or a positive self-esteem. Her self-esteem will influence her willingness to try new things and the way she relates to others. By the time a child is six, she has a pretty good idea of her own worth.

How is self-esteem developed? What are the basic influences that determine how a child feels about herself? Parents and other caregivers such as teachers and day-care personnel influence self-esteem. Of course, parents influence a child's feelings about herself more than anyone else. This is how God meant it to be. Christian parents are in the business of making people according to God's plan. Therefore, you must remember that self-esteem is developed in your children through how they perceive that you feel about them. In other words, children develop an image of themselves by observing their parents' actions, words, tone of voice, and so forth as their parents relate to them. Actions, words, and attitudes become the mirrors in which the child sees herself. If parental words, actions, and attitudes are demeaning, she has trouble liking herself. On the other hand, if parents show positive regard for their child, she will enjoy being the person she is.

The first step in developing a good self-image in your child is to have a good image of yourself. A parent who does not feel good about himself has trouble communicating positively with his child. Are you comfortable with the person you know yourself to be?

If you do not like the person you are, try the following:

1. Accept the fact that God loves and accepts you. Thank Him for accepting you.

2. Determine what you want to change about yourself and work on changing what is in your power to change. Recognizing a weakness is the first step. Then, determine definite action you will take to deal with your bad temper, for example. Tell yourself that you are responsible for the way you act. Take responsibility for yourself.

3. Refrain from putting yourself down. Graciously accept the compliments of others about your cooking, the way you dress, and so forth. You can agree with the truth about something you have done without being vain or boastful.

4. Look for positive aspects of who you are and accept them. Qualities such as sincerity, honesty, or kindness

may be part of who you are. Whatever your qualities, recognize and nurture them as you attempt to deal with your faults.

The second step in developing a good self-image in your child is to accept your child as the gift that she is. Accepting your child as a gift opens the possibility for communicating your joy and thankfulness that she is yours. To feel wanted and loved is your child's first right. Feeling wanted and loved is also indispensable to a good self-image.

The remainder of the discussion on needs will lead you to see how other areas are related to building a good self-image in your child.

Acceptance

Young children need to know that it is OK for them to be who they are. Some children grow up with the perception that they were never really accepted by their parents. Perhaps they grow up with a deep-seated dissatisfaction with being a boy or girl. Girls seem particularly vulnerable to this in American society. Sometimes it seems that both men and women, in general, prefer having boys. Several years ago I knew an attractive young woman who, though pretty and intelligent, had trouble being a woman. The problem lay in her father's expressed wishes that she had been a boy. Somehow, she had received his message and was still attempting to be "his boy." She was confused and troubled because she did not really feel accepted by a person she deeply loved.

As parents we run the risk of putting on our children a burden or responsibility they cannot bear. Parents are tempted to try to accomplish through their children things they themselves have never been able to do. Children pay the bill emotionally for such action. This is a way of saying to a child that she is not acceptable. Parents may want their child to be the star athlete they were never able to be because of "circumstances" beyond their control or to be a great pianist or dancer.

Children differ vastly in ability according to heredity and the training of environment. They cannot change the fact that they are male or female. Neither do some children come with coordination necessary to accomplish great sports feats.

What children are physically, intellectually, and emotionally depends on their parents. They inherit intellectual, physical, and personality traits from parents and other ancestors. Sex, hair color, eye color, body structure, and many other factors are controlled by parents and heredity. You can give your child a good environment for developing, but she can never go beyond the boundaries set for her by heredity in her development.

The important issue is to attempt to discover the gifts of your child and help her develop in areas where there is real potential. This does not mean to totally neglect areas where she may have less talent. Rather let your child's gifts determine what is really important to you. Every child has the right to be accepted on the basis of who she is. Her worth should never depend on a parent's unfulfilled dream or unrealistic expectation.

Some expectant parents are strongly convinced that their first child has to be a boy, while others want a girl and would seem disappointed otherwise. The sex of a child is determined at the moment the sperm fertilizes the egg or ovum. Since that is true, it would seem that a commitment to truly accept the sex of the child should come before an attempt to have a child is made. While couples may know several months in advance through medical technology what sex their child is, it would not be wise to predetermine the sex of the child we have even if that were possible and acceptable. Children are a gift from God, and some things about the nature of the gift should be left to the discretion of the Giver. For the Christian, God should be allowed to determine what is best. To really love a child is to accept her unconditionally—as God has given.

Trust

A young child needs to know that she can trust those who take care of her. Trust in parents is basic to life and is the basis for trust in the love and dependability of God. Trust for your child will be communicated as you lovingly meet her basic needs for tenderness, food, and warmth. Being consistent about what you say and do is a powerful lesson in trust for your child. Because of the independability of circumstances, parents should be very cautious about making promises they may not be able to keep. If you develop a pattern of making promises you cannot fulfill, your child will soon sense that nothing you say or do is dependable.

Giving your child a model for trust is a vital part of doing what is best for her. She will need trust throughout her life as she relates to a complex network of other people. She will be able to live comfortably and successfully only as she is able to trust herself and others in human relationships. She will also need to trust if she is ever to know God in a meaningful way. The beginning of this trust in God is through her relationship to you, her parents.

A child's ability to trust, like a sense of self-worth, is acquired through experiences which reinforce the trustworthiness of the parent. God planned that your child learn the meaning of trust through you. Through providing a dependable environment and relationship, you are preparing your child for her future—a future in which trust is absolutely essential.

Guidance

God gave children parents so that they may learn how to live in a world of people and things. The young child's void of understanding of her world is almost overwhelming to her parents. She must learn everything about how to get along in her world! She needs guidance, and this responsibility also falls primarily on parents.

Like many parents, I have often felt that it would have been easier if every child came with an instruction book. But that is not the case. They must receive guidance through instruction as they experience their world.

There seem to be a few basic lessons parents must help

a child learn about getting along in her world. Here are some simple statements you may want to think about:

1. Every child must sense that she is of worth before she can recognize the importance of others, their feelings, and rights.

2. Every child must experience kindness, consideration, and love before she can express these attitudes toward others.

3. Every child must be protected from situations which will be physically harmful to her or others. For instance, throwing objects should not be allowed. Likewise, household cleaners, etc. should be put out of reach because children do not realize they are dangerous even if they are told.

Security

Children need to feel safe. This need has to do with the feeling that someone is in charge, and they will be protected or cared for whatever happens. Children who do not have a dependable environment with some type of "normal" routine can become fearful or insecure. Children need the security that boundaries or limits give. Children expect adults to be in charge and are very fearful when they feel adults have completely relinquished their responsibility to keep them safe. While too many limits or rules stifle the child, the absence of rules or limits makes her fearful or insecure.

Dependence/Independence

Rearing children is a dynamic process. Parents must be

aware of their child's growing abilities while understanding her limitations. The young child needs a balance of dependence and independence in her life. Parents can meet this need by encouraging and allowing their child to do what she can for herself. This growth in independence can take all kinds of practical forms, involving the child in the care of her own needs as well as being a helper around the house, according to her ability. While growing in the ability to do things on her own, she will still be dependent on you for other needs.

Patience must be the parents' ruling attitude in this process of growth. Children need freedom to do for themselves whenever possible while not being rushed or judged according to adult standards of performance. Sincere encouragement will do wonders to produce a helpfully independent attitude in your child.

Discipline

A major ingredient in helping a child learn to relate properly to God and others is discipline. Parents must accept their role as the persons who will determine what is and is not acceptable in the behavior of their child. Appropriate methods of dealing with behavior must be chosen and used consistently. Young children need and want rules which are fair and consistent. They want parents to be "in charge." Children who are not reared in homes where there are certain expectations feel that parents do not really love them enough to set limits. The final chapter is devoted to a discussion of discipline.

As you have seen, loving your child is a very complicated thing. Simply stated, it is doing what is best for her. But doing what is best means recognizing what she needs and meeting those needs. This type of love will go a long way toward helping your child relate positively to God and to others.

To Think About

1. Briefly define parent love.

2. Scan through the chapter and list and briefly define or describe some of the needs parent love deals with.

6

I Think You're Special

Some of my fondest memories of our earliest attempts at parenting have to do with helping our children know they are very special to us. When Nathan was just toddling, my wife would say, "Nathan, if all the little boys in the world lined up and I could choose anyone I wanted, I would choose you." Later she changed her wording to a question, "Nathan, if all the little boys in the world lined up and I could choose anyone I wanted, do you know who I would choose?" At that young age Nathan could not conceptualize the idea of all the little boys in the world lining up, but he understood from the words of his mother that he is very special. Even at that young age he replied with a happy *me* to her question.

While there are many gifts parents can give their children, there is no rival to the sense of "specialness" a child can receive from them.

A child's feelings about himself will color his feelings about others and God. Self-image is at the very foundation of relationships. Jesus implied as much in his summation of the Commandments in Matthew 22:37-39.

Thou shalt love the Lord thy God with all thy heart, and with all thy soul, and with all thy mind. This is the first and great commandment. And the second is like unto it, Thou shalt love thy neighbour as thyself.

This lofty concept of putting God first and loving our neighbor as ourself has its foundation in the theological premise that God is worthy of worship, that others have great worth, and that I—an individual—have great worth to God, to others, and to myself. The beginning for such a relationship with God and others is an acceptance of myself as a person of worth.

Basically, life is a matter of keeping relationships in the proper perspective. We are to love God supremely and live in obedience to His will. His will involves not only accepting His teachings mentally but applying those teachings to our relationships with others. The application of God's will to relationships must come from within— from a person who feels he is of value as a person.

At this point in my life, my experiences have led me to feel that building a good self-image or self-esteem in a child is the first and most crucial task of parenting.

What Is Self-Image?

Self-image is the way persons feel about or view themselves. All persons have an overall view or attitude toward themselves as persons. We may be basically satisfied or dissatisfied with who we are. We may highly value or think little of ourselves as persons; thus, the image "I'm

OK" or "I'm not OK." We develop such attitudes and values concerning self through the mirrors in our lives.

Self-images are formed early in life but can be altered to some degree, positively or negatively, through the years. Basically, though, how one thinks of himself as a child is how he thinks of himself as an adult. Obviously, then, self-image affects almost everything we do in life and will in turn affect our children and our children's children.

Building a Healthy Self-Image

There are at least three areas you should be concerned about in attempting to build a healthy self-image in your child: body and physical attractiveness, sense of accomplishment or defeat, and significant others.

Body and Physical Attractiveness

How children view their bodies is important. For instance, children with physical handicaps must often learn to accept their bodies and to cope with the fact that they cannot participate in some of the activities of children who are physically normal. Such children face the real danger of being emotionally crippled or damaged if parents do not give them every opportunity to be as independent as they can be. Handicapped children need acceptance, but not pity.

The child's general physical health is another important factor in the development of self-image. The child whose energy is not constantly drained by illness is more likely to have curiosity and be involved in exploring the world.

A child's self-image is closely related to physical health and stamina.

Appearance is one of the most obvious areas of the child's physical situation which may greatly affect self-image. To make physical appearance the basis of a child's acceptance is unfair and cruel. James Dobson in *Hide or Seek* makes this truth painfully clear: "The most highly valued personal attribute to our culture is physical attractiveness. . . . We adults respond very differently to an unusually beautiful child than to a particularly unattractive one, and that difference has a profound impact on a developing personality."[6]

Children need and deserve total acceptance regardless of their physical abilities or inabilities, attractiveness or unattractiveness. They are created as persons of worth and have the right to personal respect and dignity.

Sense of Accomplishment or Defeat

Young children are doers. They learn by doing. Fitzhugh Dodson contends in *How to Parent* that giving children freedom to do things within their limitations builds a positive view of self.[7]

Children who are constantly being told that they are dumb or stupid because their work does not meet adult standards may soon conclude that they are losers. Instead of emphasizing their limitations, parents need to show interest in and praise for the things they can do. Children, like adults, feel good about themselves when they accomplish a challenging task. Turning over, sitting up, crawling, walking, running, jumping, talking, singing, putting a puzzle together for the first time, tying shoes, buttoning, zipping, and using the potty are major accomplishments for the young child and should be treated as such. Such achievements speak not only of increasing independence but also of a growing awareness that the child can do important things.

Parents who insist on doing everything for their children rob them of opportunities to learn and to see themselves as growing persons. Parents should encourage work and play activities that are within children's abilities. As parents, we need to let children feel they are really helping us. Some examples of chores young children can do are washing dishes, emptying trash cans, picking up toys, straightening their rooms, and helping in the yard. Allowing children to do these tasks will take more time and trouble than doing them ourselves. But the completion of such tasks will make an important contribution to the children's feelings of self-worth. Successfully performing tasks helps children learn to trust in their own capabilities.

Often parents and other adults make unrealistic demands on a child. These demands are not adults' efforts to be sadistic or unkind to the child; they occur because the adults do not understand him. Adults often have difficulty remembering that their child is not a miniature adult. This is true in regard to his physical, emotional, intellectual, and spiritual being.

The child's thought processes are not the same as those of an adult and limit the ability to respond as an adult for two basic reasons. First, the brain is not fully developed, and the young child is unable to master adult concepts. Second, a young child is limited in experiences and, therefore, cannot understand many of the things adults do.

Because of these reasons, the young child's thinking is limited. Two words seem to best describe the thinking processes of preschoolers: literal and concrete. The parent must constantly be alert because of these limitations. Young children take everything that is said literally because they are not yet able to think abstractly. Young children have difficulty understanding that words have symbolic as well as literal meanings.

Because young children think in concrete terms, they deal with the here and now. Preschoolers have difficulty understanding yesterday and tomorrow. Both time and distance have little meaning to them. Grandmother and Grandfather's house may be thought to be just a few miles away when in actuality it is several hundred miles away.

Parents' unwillingness to accept these thought process limitations may undo the very things they want to accomplish with their child. As parents, we need to remember not to push a child to accomplish beyond his ability, or we will frustrate and discourage him. When these "not OK" feelings surface, the child's self-esteem suffers.

Significant Others

The third and most important mirror in the development of the self-image is how significant others, especially parents, view the child. No one's opinions and attitudes are more important to a child than those of his parents. As parents, your view of your child in large measure determines how he feels about himself. Wayne Oates in *On Becoming Children of God* wrote: "The self-image of a child forms around the estimates those near to him have of him. It also grows in terms of the comparisons they make of him with other persons."[8]

Parents are mirrors for children. Words, slaps, hugs, looks of anger, surprise, or joy vividly reflect the ways parents feel about children at certain times. Children have an uncanny ability to understand whether the mirrors they are watching say they are OK or not OK.

As parents, we must realize that while all our experiences with our children are not and cannot be pleasant, the majority of them should be. Most of our experiences with our children will be positive and pleasant ones if we keep in mind a few basic issues.

● Accept your child unconditionally. Allow him to be himself—to be a child. Children are of worth because God made them in His own image, and your child is a special gift from God to you.

● Emphasize the positive things in your child's life. Pay attention to accomplishments, and let your child know you are proud of him. Show understanding when he fails, but help him to realize that to fail at one thing does not mean he is a failure at life.

● Be the kind of person your children will be glad to tell your grandchildren about. You can show no greater love and respect for your children than to give them a good example to follow.

"Ways to Say It"

Parents basically determine the climate in which the ego of the child is developed. An understanding of himself and feelings about who he is are formulated through the channels of communication available to the child. Parents can use these channels of communication to build a positive self-image in their child. There are at least three areas of communication which are vitally important.

Emotional Climate

Parents, and perhaps the mother more than the father, can set the emotional climate which is conducive to healthy, growing relationships. In the early years of life, children seem to be particularly sensitive to feelings. Research has shown that the unborn child is sensitive to the feelings of the mother and is affected by her emotional state.

While family relationships will have emotional stress and tension, the child should never be left in doubt about the stability of his home. While children should not be protected from every argument or expression of anger, they should be able to experience the resolution and reconciliation of feelings. A child who grows up without experiencing family conflict will be ill-equipped to face the real world of conflict in personal relationships. The important fact to remember is to never let the importance of the child and his security be in doubt.

When anger is expressed in relation to your child a good rule to remember is: *Deal with the child's action, not personality.* You can be honest with your feelings without damaging the personality of your child. Which one of the following examples illustrates this?

"You little monster, you just broke my favorite vase."
"Brian, I'm very upset because you broke the vase. You must put the ball away."

Obviously, calling Brian a monster does not help his self-image. He senses that a parent's anger is directed toward him personally and not toward what he did. The second example deals with the issue of a broken vase and attempts not to add a broken child to the casualty list. The second example allows for the expression of anger in a legitimate way.

Another important point to remember when negative emotions are expressed is to be ready for reconciliation. Do not let the encounter end without affirming the child. If your child turns to you for consolation be ready to hold him and assure him of your love.

Words Are Important

Assuming that your child knows he is important to you is a dangerous thing. Your child needs to hear you say that he is important to you. Words which confirm his worth are especially meaningful when there is a consistency with the emotional climate. Where there is consistency between words and actions the child is not left to "figure out" the puzzle of how you really feel about him. Be careful that your tone of voice does not betray you. If you are irritated, why not say it and be honest? The other option is to pretend you are not irritated with his action and take the chance of saying one thing with your tone of voice and another with your words. This double message confuses your child.

You can encourage your child's growth by being aware of progress and encouraging your child. For example, talking to him about sitting up, crawling, or walking encourages him to trust his own abilities and shows your pleasure with his progress. The earlier you start encouraging and complimenting your child the more likely you are to get into the habit of talking to him in a positive way: a good habit! Just as you are training him to think about himself in positive ways you also need to train yourself from the time he is young to speak to him in positive ways.

Physically

Being a good parent is very time-consuming. While parenting should not consume all your time and energy, it will make definite demands. Giving yourself physically to play with your child can say a great deal about his value and your delight in his company.

My children have always had numerous toys for different stages of their development. I have often felt that they have had much more than they needed or could ever use. In rearing my children, I have discovered that the child's favorite plaything cannot be bought and presented in pretty paper and ribbon. I have discovered that I, the parent, am the favorite "toy." Playing house, horse, school, and wrestling are experiences which will make an indelible impression about your child's worth. More than toys, you must give your child yourself. There is no substitute for "you."

There are other ways you can enhance your child's good feelings about himself through physical contact. Do not overlook these ego boosters: touching, hugging, smiling, and so forth. Communicate your regard for your child physically. Make it a point each day to tell him physically how very important he is to you.

To Think About

1. Why do you think self-esteem is an essential bridge to a positive relationship with God and others? Discuss this question with your husband or wife in light of Matthew 22:37-39.
2. What are some practical things you can do to build a positive self-image in your child?
   a.
   b.
   c.
   d.

7

Communication:
Lifeline of Relationships

One of my goals as a parent is to create an atomosphere in which my children will feel free to talk to me about anything or ask any kind of question. If the lines of communication are open when children are young, there is a good possibility that positive, honest relationships can be maintained throughout life. Communication keeps relationships alive. Communication patterns set in childhood tend to persist in adulthood.

Since so much of adult relationships depends on open communication it seems important to develop good communication skills while one is young. And what of the most sublime form of communication possible to a human being—prayer? What if human relationships with parents do not foster open, honest expression? Surely, this will hinder the openness and freedom God gives us in prayer. How can one express all his needs to God in prayer if he has never been able to talk openly about his needs with human parents? And if good communication is not modeled in the home, how can a child develop a good pattern of communication for a future home?

What Is Communication?

In its most basic form, communication is the process of giving and receiving a message. Good communication takes place when the message given is understood by the person receiving it the way the person giving it intended it. Clear enough? In communication there is a sender and a receiver. Often a person is both a sender and a receiver in a conversation. I speak, and I listen to you. I observe you even as I speak to you. You can "talk" to me without saying a word through expressions on your face.

There are two basic purposes the Christian parent should seek to accomplish through communication with a child:

(1) To bring about mutual understanding and respect, to build an empathetic relationship and,

(2) To give instruction concerning goals and expectations, religious, social, or others.

Ways of Communicating

What are ways to communicate with children. First, and most obvious, is *talking*. We send messages through the words we speak. Words are the carriers of meaning. But how difficult it is to help others understand what we want our words to say to them. Just the other day I heard a woman say, "I wish I could communicate more clearly." I could sense by the expression on her face and the tone of her voice that she was having difficulty getting others to understand what she was trying to say.

Perhaps we rely too heavily on words alone to communicate the messages we want to send to others. We talk so much that we may need to talk less and concentrate more on what we intend to say and how to say it in a way which communicates best. Someone has observed that *every day* each of us probably speaks enough words to fill an average book of thirty to fifty thousand words!

Words are important. They are particularly important when spoken to a young child. Words can harm or help, tear down or build up, dishearten or encourage. As you consider what you say and how you say it to your child, consider these words of wisdom:

> Let the words of my mouth . . . be acceptable in Thy sight, O Lord (Ps. 19:14, NASB).
> How delightful is a timely word! (Prov. 15:23, NASB).
> "And I say to you, that every careless word that men shall speak, they shall render account for it in the day of judgment" (Matt. 12:36, NASB).

We also communicate in *nonverbal* ways. These nonverbal methods, methods not using words, can enhance or compliment the meaning of words. As a matter of fact, the nonverbal methods are often the interpretation of what we are trying to say. For example, a hug or touch can bring real feeling or meaning to such words as *I love you.* A smile, a stare, an angry look, arms folded, gesture with hands, and tone of voice are other ways to help words say what we intend to communicate. Or we can communicate through these without the use of words.

It is important to remember that the young child is

more sensitive to feelings and nonverbal communication than she is to words. This means that we should be in touch with what we are communicating to our child through facial expressions, tone of voice, gestures, and so forth. This is where communication can get tricky.

Let's look at an example of how communication can break down. It is possible that you are angry over something your child has done. Instead of admitting your anger and telling her you are angry over what has happened you determine you will remain sweet and pleasant and pretend nothing has happened. She senses from your feeling that something is wrong and comes to you for reassurance. You attempt to reassure her with the words she wants to hear, but your body is tense; your vocal tone shows anger. A problem! Either you must determine to share your anger in a helpful way, or you will be communicating soothing words, such as *I love you*, in harsh tones!

Listening is a vitally important part of parent-child communication. One of the most frustrating parts of parenting very young children is that they cannot talk. They cannot tell us why they are crying, what they want, or where they hurt. Probably one of the most frustrating things about being a child is having a parent who will not really listen to what she is saying. How can we hope to build a relationship of understanding with our child if we do not understand her? How can we understand her feelings if we never listen—listen without interrupting, without judging, or correcting.

What Good Parent-Child Communication Is

Good communication presupposes a real respect for the child as a person. Out of that respect grows a willingness to listen to ideas and feelings. Good communication involves a relationship of trust in which the parent can be open and honest with the child and vice versa. Respect and trust are the two foundations for good communication.

Good communication between parent and child is basically the parent's responsibility. It begins with some very basic understandings about their relationship. As a parent, you realize that first, my child is an important person. Second, what he thinks and says are important to me. Third, good communication will build our relationship, but bad communication can destroy it. Fourth, good communication requires real love and honesty. Fifth, I must model good communication for my child.

Essentially, good communication involves a proper mixture of talking, listening, and nonverbal methods to get the message heard in the way it was intended.

Guidelines for Good Communication

Here are some guidelines to help you decide what is really essential in communicating with your child.

1. *Determine what you want your child to think about himself.* This thought takes us back to our earlier discussion of self-esteem. Make a commitment to God and yourself that you will not betray the ideal of helping your child see himself as a person of

worth. Use all available methods of communication to tell him he is loved and important to you and to God.

2. *Listen with your heart as well as your ears.* Cultivate the ability to look at life from your child's perspective. Try to recall your childhood and the difficulties of being small. Be cautious about laughing at your child's feelings or teasing about things that are important to him. Listen for what your child is feeling beyond the words he is saying.

3. *Be honest.* Develop a pattern of being honest and open with your child. If there is information he does not need or cannot handle, do not force-feed him. Tell him the truth in the doses he is able to take. Speak to him about your mistakes. If you make a mistake in the way you have handled a problem with him, apologize to him. This undergirds the idea that your child is an important person. He will forgive you, and you will further cement your relationship.

4. *Do what you say.* One of the major flaws in parenting is the difference in the ideals we teach our children and our personal action. Our words mean very little if they are not complemented by our actions. The parent whose personal life is punctuated with dishonesty has a difficult task in communicating to the child that honesty is really "the best policy." Words without action are just that: empty words with no meaning.

5. *Talk on your child's eye level.* Many children grow

up thinking parents' faces look like kneecaps. The voice they hear seems to come from somewhere above but all they see is kneecaps! How much better to bend or to stoop down to your child's eye level and talk face-to-face, person to person. Remember, your kneecaps cannot smile at your child. Bending to their level has other benefits. It reduces the threat of your large size in communicating. The child is much more at ease to talk when you have reduced your size a bit.

6. *Use words he can understand.* Remember that your child is literal minded and takes what you say at face value. Attempt to simplify what you want to say so that your child can understand what you are saying. Some of us work in technical jobs which call for complicated words. We tend to bring those words and that manner home with us and our child. Simplify.

7. *Avoid communication traps.* There are several hindrances to good communication we need to avoid. Here are a few of them.

(1) Assuming you understand when you really do not. This can lead to answering questions that are not being asked. If you are not sure you really understand, ask your child to talk further and help you understand.

(2) Attacking your child instead of the problem. This results from a wrong use of anger on our part. The solution is to be honest about your feelings in a constructive way.

(3) Sending double messages. Be aware of your feelings and work on being honest with them. Use nonverbal communication to help you say what you need to say but avoid the conflict between what your words and your body are saying. This is confusing to your child.

(4) Assuming that silence is bad. Many times a look, a smile, or a touch can say more than a hundred words. One of the pitfalls of parent-child communications is that parents, in general, talk too much. We overdose our children on so many words that they have trouble understanding when we are serious about what we say.

(5) Listening is what children are supposed to do. Perhaps the biggest trap in communication with our children is the assumption that talking is what parents do, and listening is what children do. This kind of communication breaks down relationships because the parent is requiring the child to understand him but he is not willing to understand the child. Talking and listening are improved if both are allowed to do them.

What Communication Is All About

The day-to-day messages we send our children should be designed to help them become what God has intended them to be. To accomplish this we must determine what message we want to communicate. We must then determine to listen, talk, touch, hug, and discipline in such a way that children will know who they are, and that who they are is important to us and God.

To Think About

1. What new insights or attitudes about communication did you gain from reading this chapter?

2. What are some practical things you can do to improve communication with your child?

8

Roots and Wings

Over the past several weeks my daughter, Kristen, has made occasional attempts to learn to ride her new bicycle. My job in this endeavor has been to "hold on" and "let go" at the appropriate signal from her. Since she has no training wheels on her bicycle, my job is very important. A typical experience on the street in front of our house goes something like this. Kristen mounts the bike while I balance it. She continues to depend on me until she is seated comfortably, positions her feet on the peddles, and brushes her hair out of her eyes. She sits for a few moments to gather her courage. Then the moment comes when she says, "Go." The wheels start turning and I walk rapidly, still holding on until she is ready for me to "let go." Once the signal to "let go" is given, she is on her own. I run along beside her, encouraging her effort and progress. As she nears the end of the ride, she signals me that it is time to "hold on" again.

Little by little, I am doing less holding on and more letting go. Soon she will be in complete control of the bicycle and will need my help no more. That is what I am working for and will be happy for her when her skills will have developed sufficiently to let her ride unaided. You might say I am working myself out of a job.

Dependence—Independence

The human infant is the most dependent of all babies born into the world. In God's plan, the human baby needs more attention than any of the babies born to animals in the created order. You will be more aware of this fact if you think of the things a baby cannot do for himself during the first few years of life! This is by design for the child to have time and opportunity to develop significant relationships of trust with adults and feel secure in who he is and in his abilities. During these early years the child is developing a root system—something to ground him and stabilize him for his life among other people.

During these early years the child is also beginning to "sprout wings." He is learning to become more and more independent of parents so that when he needs to "leave the nest" he is able to "fly" on his own. The parents' role in this process is to provide the soil for roots and to teach the fine art of flying.

The Need for Roots

We have all seen roots. We have noticed them on weeds we have pulled, shrubs we have planted, and foods we have eaten. As a matter of fact, some foods we eat are the root part of the plant—potatoes, carrots, radishes—just to name a few. But what is a root? What is its function? Webster defines "root" as the part of a plant that is usually below the ground. It holds the plant in position, draws nourishment from the soil, and stores food.

The three functions mentioned here offer an intriguing possibility for what roots mean to the child's life.

Roots provide stability in the child's life. The roots of a plant grow into and "grab hold" of the soil. Transplanting shrubs has taught me that moving a plant from one place to another is not an easy process. It seems that the roots do not want to turn loose of where they are. These roots provide a sense of stability that keep the plant standing during strong winds and storms.

Life brings assaults of discouragement, change, and temptation. The person whose life has been rooted in good soil will weather the storm. Those who do not have a good root system will not endure. Quite simply, the child who is genuinely loved and cared for is the child who will have this sense of stability in his life. He can trust those closest to him and because of this trust learn to trust God and others.

Roots take in nutrients for growth in the child's life. As Webster indicates, another purpose of a root is to provide a system for carrying nourishment to the plant. The child who has a root system of love, who feels good about who she is, can freely open his life to the nurturing of his parents. His "root system" readily receives the nourishment parents provide in the soil for him. This nurturing is provided to grow the child to a maturing, loving, happy individual who can meet the tests of life.

The Bible often uses the concept of a plant to describe the nurturing of a child to love God and His ways. The parent is the loving nurse who gently cares for the tender little plant. The words *nursery* and *nurture* have a close relation to the word *nurse*—one who nurtures and protects. In Ephesians Paul reminds parents to give attention to nurturing (nursing) their children to serve the Lord, "Bring them up in the nurture and admonition of the Lord" (6:4).

To summarize what has been said to this point about the root system and the parents' role: First, the parent is to provide the root system of love and trust in order to give the child stability. Second, the parent is to continue to provide proper spiritual nurture so that the child's root system can draw in the nourishment and help the child grow into the person God wants him to be.

Roots provide storage for later use in the child's life. A plant's root stores food for the time when additional nourishment for growth and survival will be needed. There is a real sense in which the lessons children learn in life have a long-term application. They must, as adults, draw from the "root system" of wisdom, courage, love, and faith which was provided when they were children. The experiences of love and faith are "stored up" as resources for life and its challenges. The values which are learned can be drawn upon in crucial times of decision in later years.

What a wonderful thing to look back and to see the meaning and continuity of life and to realize that we have roots. Those of us who have such roots continue to be blessed in thousands of ways through our adult years. Such a life is described by the psalmist:

He shall be like a tree planted by the rivers of water, that bringeth forth his fruit in his season; his leaf also shall not wither; and whatsoever he doeth shall prosper (Ps. 1:3).

The Need for Wings

The need for a growing sense of independence in the child's life comes from two basic facts. One day she will need to make decisions of her own and take responsibility for those decisions. She will never learn to live as a responsible person if someone else makes all of her decisions for her. Second is the fact of our mortality. To put it bluntly: parents will die, and the child must learn to live without parents. That sounds rather harsh, but, nevertheless, it is true. Parents will not always be around to encourage or advise. So the loving thing to do is to help the child "sprout some wings." She will need to learn to do more for herself, to trust her own abilities, to trust God and not her parent as the main focus of her life. As a parent, you need to work yourself out of a job. Not many of us, as parents, are ready for this task.

A mother of a kindergarten child lingered at the classroom door on the first day of school. Tears came to her eyes as she watched her son become involved in an early activity. Seeing that she was having difficulty, a school administrator asked about the problem. He asked if the child had given problems in coming. He then saw the boy making a rapid adjustment to the situation. That wasn't the problem. Then, with a degree of puzzlement, he asked the mother what was wrong. She responded, "I'm crying because he's not crying to go back home with me."

Some parents tend to feel that they can control the love of their child for them so long as that child is dependent on them. The opposite is more nearly the truth. The parent who insists on possessing the child is not relating to the child as a person who has a right to think his own thoughts and to be his own person. This child feels used and manipulated and will resent the parent for this treatment.

As parents, we need to encourage our children to develop their abilities physically, socially, intellectually, and spiritually. Here are some simple guidelines which may prove helpful:

1. *Encourage your child to try new things.*

Help him to be open to activities which will expand his understanding of himself and his world. Provide opportunities which will challenge your child but do not overtax his energy with too many things at one time. For example, expose your child to educational toys, puzzles, books, games appropriate for his age. Help him to have a variety of experiences.

2. *Allow your child to do what he can for himself.*

Be aware of your child's growing abilities and allow him to do what he can for himself. As he is able to take off his coat, encourage him to do it. As he is able to button, zip, tie, and brush, allow him to be involved. Encourage his helpfulness and comment on how big he is becoming.

3. *Give only the help your child needs.*

Sometimes we become partners in an activity a child can only partially complete. Let him do what he can, and we can help do what he cannot. The problem here is that we often become impatient and insist on doing the whole activity. This robs the child of doing what he can and from observing us so he can learn more about how to do the part he cannot do.

Some parents are so insistent on doing for their children that they actually retard their progress. It is known that some children have been slow to learn to talk because there was no need for them to learn. Parents were always anticipating their need and supplied what they needed before the child could ask!

Gradually Letting Go

Watching children grow is a bittersweet experience. As parents, we have joy in their growth but mourn in advance the day they will be on their own. This struggle is only natural but must be resolved by the constant reminder that children are not ours to possess. They are ours only for a while, just as we were with our parents. We must teach them to be independent of us.

This struggle was graphically illustrated in our family a few years ago when Nathan was first learning to ride his bike. Cecelia, my wife, had come into the backyard where the attempts were taking place and offered to relieve me a bit. My job was essentially that described earlier with my daughter, Kristen. Nathan had been doing quite well and was eager to ride with only a minimum of help in getting on the bike and getting balanced. As I walked to another part of the yard to check on Kristen, I heard Nathan and his mother talking about roots and wings. The conversation went something like this:

Nathan: Thanks, Mom, I'm balanced; you can let go.
(There was a moment of silence.)
Nathan (voice louder): "Mom, let go."
Mom (somewhat distraught): "Nathan, I can't let go."
Nathan (louder): "Let go, I can do it."
Mom (louder): "I can't."

Sometimes letting go is hard! But when the child is capable of handling a situation, we must let go and trust that he will use what he has already learned—depend on the resources and nurturing we have been providing all along. And we must trust the work we have done to make him equal to the test.

Roots and wings provide many benefits in relationships with God and others.

Your child learns to trust himself and can make decisions about serving God and others out of a background of values that will endure. He will learn to take responsibility for himself and his decisions. He can learn to relate to others in ways that allows them to be who they are without wanting to change them.

To Think About

1. Why do you need to provide roots for your child?
2. Why does your child need wings?
3. How will giving your child roots and wings build bridges to relationships with God and others?

9
Discipline/Positive Guidance

Entire books have been written on the subject of child discipline. Many of these books are inadequate to really help the reader understand what discipline is all about. Yet, I am attempting to write about discipline in only a few pages! I confess that a thorough treatment of the many aspects of discipline would require much more consideration than I will give here. But please bear in mind that the reason why I write is not to give you the "last word" on any of the subjects covered in this book. My purpose is to help you identify the major concerns in building bridges on which your child can safely cross to relationships with God and others.

There are many books which propose to cover questions about discipline. Any book needs to be read with a degree of caution. No one has the absolute answer on any subject, especially discipline.

The suggestions in the following pages will help you identify some of the major issues in discipline. Principles will be stated which can help you evaluate what you read and whether or not it will apply to your situation.

What Is Good Discipline?

How do you define discipline? Many parents think of discipline only in terms of punishment. Such things as spanking and verbal reprimands would be some of the kinds of punishment used as "discipline." But that way of thinking is much too narrow and dangerous. It is too narrow because good discipline *encourages good behavior* as well as *discourages bad behavior.* It is dangerous because it tends to deal with the bad behavior and ignore the good behavior. This teaches a child that the only successful way to get attention is through bad behavior.

I see discipline as the process of teaching a child to understand how he should act in such a way that he will gradually accept your teaching and incorporate these "acceptable" behaviors into his life. Let's explore this concept of discipline a little further.

Discipline is a process of teaching. Parents must assume that their role in discipline is that of a teacher: one who is learning yet responsible to teach one who knows much less. Discipline involves a "process" of teaching. All is not taught or learned in one lesson. The process involves many attempts to teach the same thing. The process involves persistence and patience day after day. The process is often very informal, nothing like a formal classroom setting. The setting in the early years will most likely be the house where you live. The activities through which you teach will be the normal interactions of family life, such as changing diapers, feeding, playing, or working. Children learn best what you expect through teaching-learning experiences you have in routine activities of the day. A strong example of this concept is given in Deuteronomy 6:4-9.

> Hear, O Israel: the Lord our God is one Lord: And thou shalt love the Lord thy God with all thine heart, and all thy soul, and all thy might. And these words, which I command thee this day, shall be in thine heart. And thou shalt teach them diligently unto thy children, and thou shalt talk of them when thou sittest in thine house, and when thou walkest by the way, and when thou liest down, and when thou risest up. And thou shalt bind them for a sign upon thine hand, and they shall be as frontlets between thine eyes. And thou shalt write them upon the posts of thy house, and on thy gates.

Discipline involves expectations. Good discipline lets the child know what is expected of him. A caution here: good discipline does not expect a three-year-old to act like a ten-year-old. So expectations should consider what a child is capable of doing or the way he is capable of acting. Some parents expect too much of young children. For example, they expect their curious toddler to understand that valuables within his reach are not to be touched! The toddler needs to explore. He is learning. The parents need to put away what they do not want him to handle rather than creating a fight every time Johnny touches the valuable piece of porcelain.

As your child grows, he will be more able to understand the reason why he can or cannot do certain things, such as climb on the back of a chair. However, the first two years or so involve protecting him from himself. He does not understand why such an act is dangerous.

Saying in a firm tone of voice, "I don't want you climbing on the chair. You must play on the floor" can communicate to your child what is acceptable and what is not. You may have to physically put your child down from the chair and speak to him several times before you make your point. Be firm, loving, and persistent, and you will finally convince your child he is to play on the floor.

Your manner of teaching is important. The situation just given above could just as easily be handled in a distructive way. The key to positive discipline is a loving manner. You can be firm, yet loving. You can be determined, yet loving. How do you stand your ground on a reasonable expectation without being unloving? You can physically remove the child from the chair without hurting him. You do not have to jerk him or be physically rough with him. You can speak to your child about his action without abusing his person or character with your words. Your tone of voice should indicate your firmness without implying your dislike for him.

Your manner with your child should help him realize that you love him and that what you do is for his good. Even though your child may protest your decision, he is comforted to know that you are in charge and that he has someone like you to care for him.

Good discipline brings change. Children whose lives are molded by love often choose the "acceptable" behaviors parents teach as their own. Much of this internalization of values takes place past the preschool years.

Nevertheless, the relationship of trust which makes such a process possible is firmly rooted in the preschool years.

The ultimate goal of good discipline is self-discipline. A self-disciplined person orders his life according to an internal set of values. The use of time, money, talents, and so forth are determined by the positive values he has chosen as his own.

Your Child Is Unique

We are all a part of the hurry-up-and-fix-it world in which we live. We tend to want quick and easy answers to every problem we face. This is also true in child discipline. Many parents think they can read one book, or several books, on the subject or listen to the advice of a friend and get all the answers they need on how to discipline their child. Going by any book or piece of advice can be a mistake. Don't many books give good direction in discipline? Certainly they do, as far as they go. As far as they go?

I do not subscribe to everything for my children in any one theory of child discipline. That's the easy way. My children are unique individuals and everything that works with one will not work with the others. What works with my friend's child may not work with mine or vice versa. Some general principles are consistent but methods of dealing with those principles may vary from child to child. Why? Because each child has his or her own personality and his or her own way of relating to rules and authority.

The parent who spends time playing with a child, observing, and evaluating the child's moods can do a much better job with discipline. This approach begins with the child and adjusts discipline methods to meet his needs. This is the concept behind the proverb writer's words: "Train up a child in the way he should go: and when he is old, he will not depart from it" (Prov. 22:6).

This approach to child discipline is often uncomfortable because it recognizes the constant need to understand the child and the need to be flexible as the child changes, and his needs change. It is dynamic, changing, growing, alive. While there are standards that remain the same, children are dealt with as individuals in light of those principles.

What Does Good Discipline Do?

There are several things good discipline will do for your child.

Good discipline will affirm your child. Children who really feel important to their parents are children whose parents deal positively with good and bad behavior. Most children would rather have parents who are too strict than to have no guidance at all. Children interpret guidance and correction as being loved. Children who have behavior problems are generally those who have an inadequate sense of self-worth. Good discipline and good self-image go hand in hand.

Good discipline will communicate what is important. Parents who give positive discipline to their children teach them what is important in life. In the day-to-day routine the child will learn from word and example what parents value. The life of the family will be structured around these values.

Good discipline will give your child a sense of limits. All children need to know what the limits are. They explore and test to find out. They are checking on you, depending on you to stop them before they go too far. Good discipline will set limits according to the need of the child.

Good discipline will give more freedom as a child can handle it. Obviously, the three-year-old can handle more freedom than a toddler. Wise parents observe the growing abilities of their children and adjust the limits outward to allow more freedom to match his growth. For example, he can be allowed to explore some books alone that the toddler may have torn to shreds if left unattended.

Good discipline prepares the child for life. The purpose of good discipline is to prepare the child to grow as a responsible person in relation to God and others. Good discipline will build bridges on which he can cross to a relationship of accepting God's standards for his life. Good discipline will guide him to use basic values in relating to others. Good discipline will also serve as a basis for developing his own principles for disciplining his own children. Good discipline prepares him for life's relationships.

General Principles for Positive Discipline

This section will be a statement of some principles of good discipline. From these principles you can formulate what will be important in guiding your child and how you will seek to accomplish your goals.

1. *The parent is the authority.* The parent must take this responsibility and use it wisely. The young child can never be in charge and decide what is best for himself. He is not equipped intellectually or emotionally to do so. Parents can discuss, explain, and allow the child to say how he feels but the ultimate decision must belong to the parent.

2. *Parents should be united.* Parents should decide together what they want to happen in a given situation and how they will deal with disobedience. They should agree to support each other and discuss differences of opinion out of the child's presence. They should agree to handle a given situation consistently and not confuse their child.

3. *All behavior has a cause.* A child acts out of needs. He needs attention and will repeat those actions which satisfy that need. He will continue to behave badly if that is the only way to get attention. His behavior may also be caused by feelings of irritability because of hunger, sleepiness, overstimulation, or a number of other things.

4. *Children tend to repeat behavior for which they are rewarded.* The principle of stimulus-response is often workable with young children. However, this can be overdone to the point of loosing its effectiveness. For instance, the child who is given candy for something she does may continue to repeat the action for the candy without any meaningful contact with parents. I much prefer giving praise or complimenting my child. The same principle is involved but a more personal involvement is required on my part.

5. *Children tend to stop behavior for which they are not*

rewarded. If a child does not receive attention from an action his need is not met. Sometimes ignoring an action is enough. Sometimes an appropriate punishment is necessary for the child to understand the action will not be tolerated. In either instance the child does not get what he wants from the behavior and will probably stop, especially if parents persist in their action toward the behavior.

6. *Discipline should accentuate the positive.* Good discipline looks for ways to stress the positive. It does not look for opportunities to reprimand. The attitude of the parent is so vital here. I must look for chances to say and do affirming things. The more positive you are, the less punishment you will have to use!

7. *Punishment should be swift and deal with the offense.* As parents, we do not need to make our child suffer for a day or a week by nagging over something she did. Deal immediately with the issue and let that be it. Young children tend to forget quickly what they are still being punished for. Suit the punishment to the act. If you have told Susan to roll the toy on the floor and she insists on banging it on furniture, take the toy from her immediately and put it away for a few minutes. You may return it to her later and tell her to use it on the floor. If she doesn't, remove the toy again.

If you have decided to use spanking as a punishment, use it only when absolutely necessary. It will be more meaningful that way and will tell your child you really will enforce what you say. But after the spanking, be open for reconciliation. Remember, *love* is the name of the game.

8. *Use the child's two major forces to guide behavior.* Your child has two strong urges which you can use to your child's advantage. First, he basically wants to please you. Let him know what pleases you and when he pleases you. This may sound ridiculous, but it is true. He needs you, and he has a strong desire to please you. Second, your child has an urge to grow up, to be big. Work to making desirable behavior a characteristic of "growing up." A compliment such as, "Thank you, Kristen, for putting the napkins on the table. You sure are growing", can do wonders for a child's behavior.

Helpful Tips for Positive Discipline

The following are a few tips derived from the principles given above. They may be helpful to you as a beginning place for disciplining your child.

1. Be friendly and firm.
2. Help your child define his feelings.
3. Avoid showing your child "how it feels." Examples: biting, kicking, and hitting.
4. Use a calm voice. This shows you are in control.
5. Give positive directions. Stress *do* instead of *don't.*
6. Reward acceptable behavior with genuine praise.
7. Encourage your child to do what he can for himself.
8. Give your child a choice only if you are willing to accept the choice.
9. Deal with your child's negative behavior and leave his personality intact.

10. Avoid nagging about a problem. Take action.

To Think About

1. What are some key ingredients of good discipline?
2. In your opinion, what is good discipline supposed to do?

Conclusion

Over two years ago, I was impressed with the need for a book on building bridges of relationships in our children's lives. I hesitated at first, and later, after beginning to outline and write, put the book on hold for several months. The reason? I was scared! Scared of such a difficult undertaking.

After reading the manuscript several times, I'm still not certain I have done exactly what I wanted to do for you, the parent. Only you can be the judge of the worth of this book. I am willing to leave that judgment to you.

What I hope you will find is encouragement to build bridges of relationship to God and others in your child's life. You have been challenged to look at yourself as the bridge-builder. Hopefully, you have made an honest attempt at this and have grown from it. You have also been guided to consider six areas (blueprints) absolutely necessary to building bridges. Discussions of these areas have not been exhaustive but have attempted to help you get a "handle" on the essential issues, so you can have a basis for decisions you will make.

There is one final thing I want you to do. As a beginning of your growing commitment as a parent, write a description of the kind of parent you want God to help you to be. Put the written statement in your Bible or some other place where you will see it often.

MOTHER
   With God's help I want to be ________________________

____

____

____

Date__________   Signed ________________________________

FATHER
   With God's help I want to be ________________________

____

____

____

Date__________   Signed ________________________________

Notes

Chapter One

1. Erik H. Erikson, *Childhood and Society,* Rev. Ed. (New York: W. W. Norton and Company, Inc., 1963), pp. 247-58.

2. Clifford Ingle, *Children and Conversion* (Nashville: Broadman Press, 1970), p. 99.

Chapter Two

3. Wesley Haystead, *You Can't Begin Too Soon* (Glendale, Calif.: International Center for Learning, 1971), p. 27.

Chapter Three

4. Kenneth Chafin, *Is There a Family in the House?* (Waco, Tex.; Word Books, 1978), p. 67.

5. Haim G. Ginott, *Between Parent and Child* (New York: Avon Books, 1965), p. 83.

Chapter Six

6. James Dobson, *Hide or Seek* (Old Tappan, N. J.: Fleming H. Revell Company, 1974).

7. Fitzhugh Dodson, *How to Parent* (New York: American Library, 1973).

8. Wayne Oates, *On Becoming Children of God* (Philadelphia: Westminister, 1969).